World Languages

Colours in
Welsh

Daniel Nunn

www.raintreepublishers.co.uk
Visit our website to find out more information about Raintree books.

To order:
☎ Phone 0845 6044371
🖨 Fax +44 (0) 1865 312263
✉ Email myorders@raintreepublishers.co.uk

Customers from outside the UK please telephone +44 1865 312262

Raintree is an imprint of Capstone Global Library Limited, a company incorporated in England and Wales having its registered office at 7 Pilgrim Street, London, EC4V 6LB – Registered company number: 6695582

Text © Capstone Global Library Limited 2013
First published in hardback in 2013
The moral rights of the proprietor have been asserted.

Edited by Daniel Nunn, Rebecca Rissman, and Sian Smith
Designed by Joanna Hinton-Malivoire
Picture research by Elizabeth Alexander
Production by Alison Parsons
Originated by Capstone Global Library Ltd
Printed and bound in China by South China Printing Company Ltd

ISBN 978 1 406 23923 2
16 15 14 13 12
10 9 8 7 6 5 4 3 2 1

British Library Cataloguing in Publication Data
Nunn, Daniel.
 Colours in Welsh. -- (World languages. Colours)
 1. Welsh language--Vocabulary--Juvenile literature.
 2. Colors--Juvenile literature. 3. Welsh language--
 Textbooks for foreign speakers--English.
 I. Title II. Series
 491.6'682421-dc23

Acknowledgements
We would like to thank Shutterstock for permission to reproduce photographs: pp.4 (© Phiseksit), 5 (© Stephen Aaron Rees), 6 (© Tischenko Irina), 7 (© Tony Magdaraog), 8 (© szefei), 9 (© Picsfive), 10 (© Eric Isselée), 11 (© Yasonya), 12 (© Nadezhda Bolotina), 13 (© Maryna Gviazdovska), 14 (© Erik Lam), 15 (© Eric Isselée), 16 (© Ruth Black), 17 (© blueskies9), 18 (© Alexander Dashewsky), 19 (© Michele Perbellini), 20 (© Eric Isselée), 21 (© Roman Rvachov).

Cover photographs reproduced with permission of Shutterstock: ... strawberry (© Stephen Aaron Rees), fish (© ... ... back ... apple reproduced ... ... mission of Shutterstock (© ... ...

... ... iths, and their ... ... he preparation of this

Every effort ... en made to contact copyright holders of material reproduced in this book ... ... will be rectified in subsequent printings if notice ... ... to the publisher.

Contents

Coch 4

Oren 6

Melyn .8

Gwyrdd 10

Glas .12

Brown 14

Pinc .16

Gwyn 18

Du 20

Dictionary 22

Index and notes 24

Coch

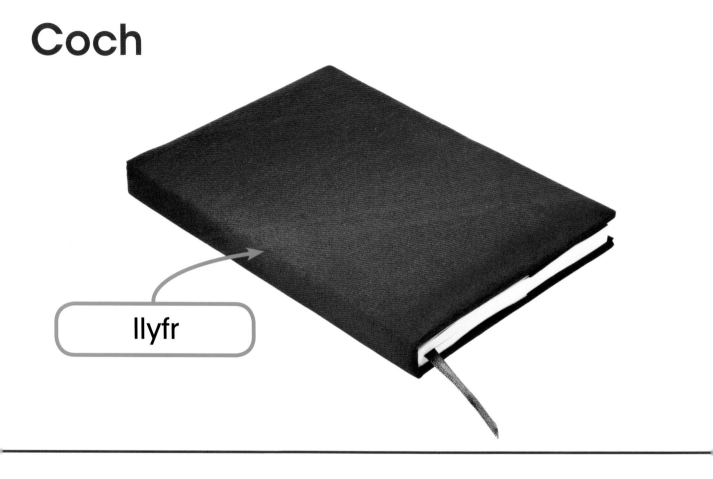

llyfr

Mae'r llyfr yn goch.

The book is red.

mefusen

Mae'r fefusen yn goch.

The strawberry is red.

Oren

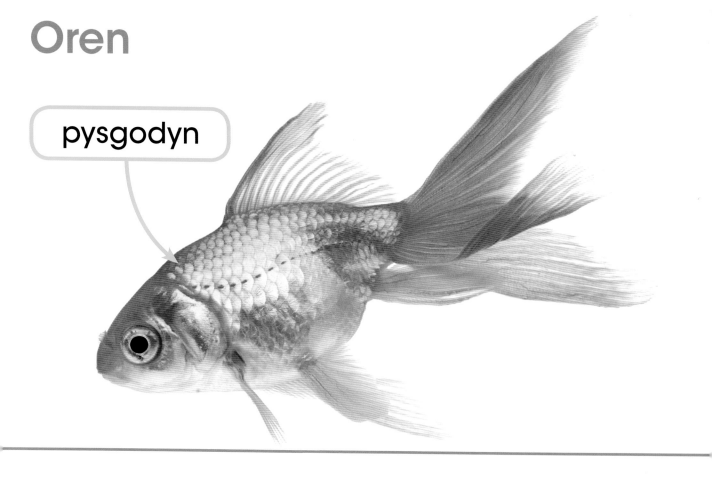

pysgodyn

Mae'r pysgodyn yn oren.

The fish is orange.

moronen

Mae'r foronen yn oren.

The carrot is orange.

Melyn

blodyn

Mae'r blodyn yn felyn.

The flower is yellow.

banana

Mae'r banana yn felyn.

The banana is yellow.

Gwyrdd

aderyn

Mae'r aderyn yn wyrdd.
The bird is green.

afal

Mae'r afal yn wyrdd.

The apple is green.

Glas

crys-t

Mae'r crys-t yn las.

The T-shirt is blue.

cwpan

Mae'r gwpan yn las.

The cup is blue.

Brown

ci

Mae'r ci yn frown.

The dog is brown.

buwch

Mae'r fuwch yn frown.

The cow is brown.

Pinc

cacen

Mae'r gacen yn binc.

The cake is pink.

het

Mae'r het yn binc.

The hat is pink.

Gwyn

llaeth

Mae'r llaeth yn wyn.

The milk is white.

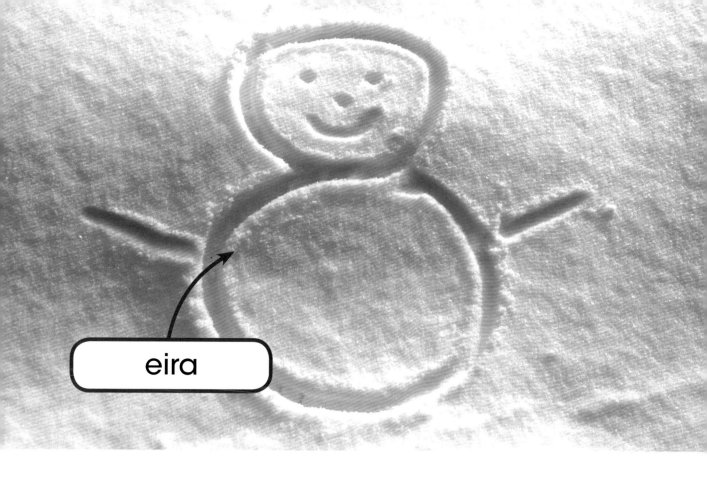

eira

Mae'r eira 'n wyn.
The snow is white.

Du

cath

Mae'r gath yn **ddu**.

The cat is **black**.

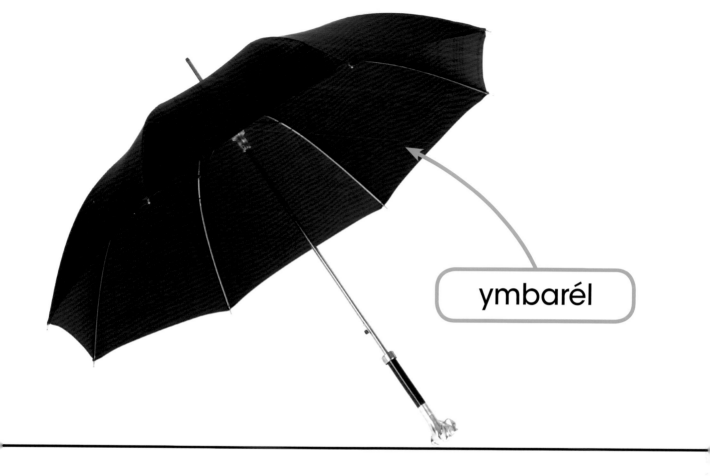

ymbarél

Mae'r ymbarél yn **ddu**.

The umbrella is **black**.

Dictionary

Welsh word	How to say it	English word
aderyn	a-der-in	bird
afal	a-val	apple
banana	ba-na-na	banana
blodyn	blo-din	flower
brown/frown	brown/vrown	brown
buwch/fuwch	bi-ooch/vi-ooch [1]	cow
cacen/gacen	ka-ken/ga-ken	cake
cath/gath	karth/garth	cat
ci	kee	dog
coch/goch	korch/gorch [1]	red
crys-t	crease-tee	T-shirt
cwpan/gwpan	coo-pan/goo-pan	cup
du/ddu	dee/thee	black
eira	aye-ra	snow
glas/las	glars/lars	blue
gwyn/wyn	gwin/win	white

Welsh word	How to say it	English word
gwyrdd/wyrdd	gwirthe/wirthe	green
het	het	hat
llaeth	thl-a-ith[2]	milk
llyfr	thl-ivr[2]	book
mae'r ... yn	my-er ... un	the ... is
mefusen/fefusen	me-vee-sen/ve-vee-sen	strawberry
melyn/felyn	mel-in/vel-in	yellow
moronen/foronen	mor-on-en/vor-on-nen	carrot
oren	or-en	orange
pinc/binc	pink/bink	pink
pysgodyn	pus-god-in	fish
ymbarél	um-ba-rel	umbrella
yn	un	is

See words in the "How to say it" columns for a rough guide to pronunciations.

[1] Note: "ch" in Welsh sounds like the "ch" in the Scottish word "loch".

[2] Note: "ll" in Welsh sounds roughly like "thl". Place your tongue as if to say "l" and hiss out of the sides of your mouth.

Index

black 20, 21

blue 12, 13

brown 14, 15

green 10, 11

orange 6, 7

pink 16, 17

red 4, 5

white 18, 19

yellow 8, 9

Notes for parents and teachers

The spelling of words in Welsh sometimes changes, depending on how the word is used in a sentence. This is why there are different spellings for many of the nouns and colours in Welsh used in this book.

24